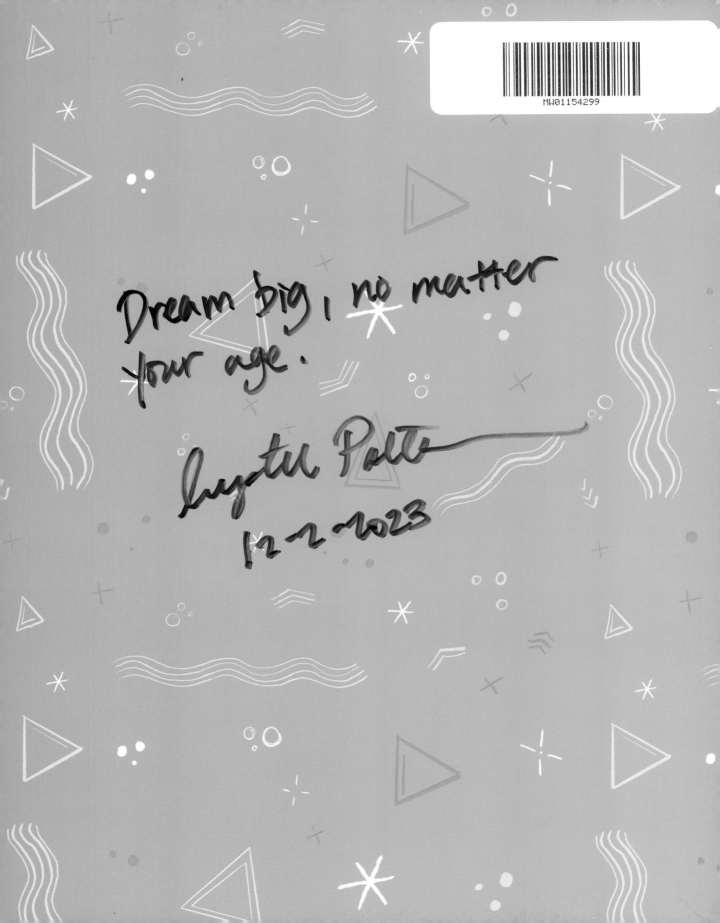

Dream big, no matter
your age.

Crystal Palte

12-2-2023

Inspired to Be...
Too Young to What?

Written by Crystel Patterson
Illustrated by Briana Young

engineer
singer
poet
chef
comedian
ceo
designer
actor

Too Young to What? by Crystel Patterson

Imprint: Independently published

ISBN-10: 1-956468-07-2

ISBN-13: 978-1-956468-07-6

Cover design by Briana Young

About this Book

The "Inspired to Be..." book series is a collection of children's books inspired by the culture, experiences, and dreams of Black people with the goal of inspiring all children.

Too Young to What? is the fourth book of the "Inspired to Be..." series.

This book is meant to inspire children to pursue their dreams, regardless of their age. Children are often told that they are too young to do certain things; however, when it comes to doing something productive that is not harmful to the child, age should not be a limitation. There are many examples of children who defied what was expected of them at their age. I hope these examples inspire the children who read this book and show them that they too, are not too young.

Oh hi, I'm Danté
and I'm feeling stressed.
I have something,
to get off my chest.

There's this awesome thing,
that I like to do.
It brings me joy,
and excitement too.

I practice each day,
so I can be great.
Yet people say,
that I need to wait.

"You're too young for that!"
Have you heard that yet?
I'm sure you have,
I'm willing to bet.

"You're too young for that!"
We are often told.
Nobody knows,
what our future holds.

Age doesn't matter,
so go spread your wings.
Kids everywhere,
do amazing things.

Like
Pe'Tehn Jackson

At the age of three,
she just couldn't wait,
to stun the world...
now isn't that great!

She learned a poem,
for a special day.
Her unique skills
blew the crowd away.

Pe'Tehn Jackson, also known as Princess Pe'Tehn, is a young poet who has been reciting and bringing poems to life in a powerful manner since the age of three.
In 2020, at the age of nine, she received the Global Child Prodigy Award in the category of poetry.

Poetry

STRONG

LEARN

Poem

Like
Mikaila Ulmer

At the age of four,
she just couldn't wait,
to help the bees...
now isn't that great!

She sells lemonade,
that's made with honey.
She's saving bees,
with her own money.

Mikaila Ulmer is the founder of Me and the Bees Lemonade, which started out as a lemonade stand in front of her home when she was four years old. Many years later, her business is booming. She donates a percentage of the profits to local and international organizations fighting hard to save honeybees.

Like
Emmanuella Samuel

At the age of five,
she just couldn't wait,
to make us laugh...
now isn't that great!

She became well known,
for a funny skit.
She's on YouTube,
her jokes are a hit.

Emmanuela Samuel, known just as Emmanuella, is a YouTube child comedian from Nigeria who got her start when she was just five years old. Since then, she has received several awards and recognition as a young comedian.

VIEWS
19,504,075

8.5M

145K [Subscribe]

10

Like
Aaron Duncan

At the age of six,
he just couldn't wait,
to make top songs...
now isn't that great!

First was calypso,
and soca came next.
He keeps winning,
his songs are the best.

Aaron Duncan is a Trinidadian calypso and soca music artist who has been winning title after title for his songs since the age of six. Calypso and soca are types of Afro-Caribbean music that originated in Trinidad and Tobago.

Like
Miles Brown

At age of seven,
he just couldn't wait,
to dance and act...
now isn't that great!

He started with dance,
then acting came next.
For his first role,
both talents he flexed.

Miles Brown, also known as Baby Boogaloo, is a talented actor, dancer, and rapper. As an actor, he landed his first movie role when he was just seven years old. He has since appeared in more than 20 movies and tv shows.

Food Donation

Donations

Donations

DON'T
wait to be GREAT

Like
Jahkil Jackson

At the age of eight,
he just couldn't wait,
to serve others...
now isn't that great!

He helped his aunty,
and gave to the poor.
Then found a way,
to keep doing more.

When Jahkil Jackson was just five years old, he helped his aunt distribute food to individuals dealing with homelessness. From then on, he knew that he wanted to do more to make a difference. At age eight, he founded Project I Am, which provides "Blessing Bags" to the homeless in Chicago.

Like
Zianna Oliphant

At the age of nine,
she just couldn't wait,
to demand change...
now isn't that great!

She bravely spoke up,
for the rights of all.
People listened,
to her tearful call.

When Zianna Oliphant was nine years old, she delivered an
unplanned and emotional speech that spoke out against
violence and made an emotional call for help.

18

worthy

BRAVE

EMPOWERED

Confident

LOVED

Like
Nyeeam Hudson

At the age of 10,
he just couldn't wait,
to spread self-love...
now isn't that great!

He was teased by kids,
for the shoes he wore.
He knew deep down,
what should matter more.

Nyeeam Hudson, also known as King Nahh, is a motivational speaker known for spreading self-love and confidence to children and their parents. When he was 10 years old, he was teased about the type of shoes he was wearing. His response got him national attention.

Like
Kelvin Doe

At age 11,
he just couldn't wait,
to solve problems...
now isn't that great!

He powered up homes,
with batteries he made.
Inventing things
is his self-taught trade.

Kelvin Doe is a self-taught engineer and inventor from Sierra Leone who began looking for ways to fix local problems with technology as an 11-year-old. In his early years, he was powering neighborhood houses with batteries made from acid, soda, and metal in a tin cup. He also built a community radio station out of recycled parts that he powered with a generator also made from reused material.

Like
Jasmine Stewart

At the age of 12,
she just couldn't wait,
to cook on stage...
now isn't that great!

Of 20 young chefs,
she was the winner.
Her winning meal:
a three-course dinner.

Jasmine Stewart is the winner of MasterChef Junior, Season 5, which is a fast-paced cooking contest for children between the ages of eight and 13. When she won first place at age 12, she became the first African American winner of MasterChef Junior.

Like me,
Danté King

I am eight years old,
and I cannot wait,
to chase my dreams...
now isn't that great!

I'll do my research
and practice each day.
I won't let age,
remain in my way.

 This story is about Danté, but what about you. Is there a
dream that you have that you would like to pursue?

Age doesn't matter, so go spread your wings.
Kids everywhere, do amazing things.

There is no limit, to what we can do.
Reach for the stars, in all you pursue.

Inspiration

This book is inspired by Machel Montano, and more specifically, the message in his debut song, "*Too Young to Soca*." Machel is the King of Soca, a genre of music originating from his home island, Trinidad. He is one of the genre's most popular artists. Machel's music career began at age seven. At age 11, he released his song "Too Young to Soca," and it became an instant hit. Despite being told he was too young to be a soca artist, he still pursued it.

In 2022, he celebrated 40 years as a musician. To this day, Machel's mission is to make soca a part of mainstream music. His dream is to see soca being enjoyed all over the world; I hope this book helps with that as well. Machel's story and the stories of the children featured in this book show us that children should be empowered to pursue their dreams—no matter how young they are.

In addition, this book is inspired by the 10 people highlighted in the story and all children who refuse to let their age limit their endless possibilities.

Brown, Miles (*Baby Boogaloo*): https://en.wikipedia.org/wiki/Miles_Brown_(actor)

Doe, Kelvin: https://gcpawards.com/blog/kelvin-doe-self-taught-engineering-prodigy/

Duncan, Aaron: https://caribbeanentertainmenthub.com/aaron-duncan-the-new-wonder-boy-of-soca

Hudson, Nyeeam: https://www.essence.com/news/10-year-old-motivational-speaker-spreads-confidence-self-love/

Jackson, Jahkil: https://inspiringyoungheroes.org/stories/jahkil/

Jackson, Pe'Tehn (*Princess Pe'Tehn*): https://bookofachievers.com/articles/reciting-poems-got-her-the-global-child-prodigy-award-just-watch-to-know-why

Montano, Machel: https://machelmontano.com/biography/

Oliphant, Zianna: https://andscape.com/features/zianna-oliphants-tearful-message-at-charlotte-city-council-meeting/

Samuel, Emmanuella: https://en.wikipedia.org/wiki/Emmanuella

Stewart, Jasmine: https://www.justchefjasmine.com/about

Ulmer, Mikaila: https://www.meandthebees.com/pages/about-us

About the Author

Photo by Kenneth McRae

Crystel is a mother to two beautiful boys, a technology consultant, and a self-published author. In January 2021, she published her first children's book, which kicked off her Inspired to Be... children's series. This series seeks to spread Black inspiration to ALL children through stories based on the culture, experiences, and dreams of Black people. Each story in the series delivers a universal message that any child can relate to and is inspired by a real person so that children will have a point of reference and can say, "If they can do that, then so can I." Crystel received her Bachelor of Science degree in Industrial Engineering and Operations Research at UC Berkeley, but her outlook on and experience with inspirational children's literature comes solely from being a mother and a seeker of inspiration. **Fun Fact: Crystel was born and raised in Trinidad, just like Machel Montano, the inspiration for this book.** To learn more about the Inspired to Be... series, visit www.crystelpatterson.com.

Make sure to check out these other books in the Inspired to Be... series: